The Summer of Love

☮

By Jim Wortham

Jim Wortham

James Wortham Publishing Company
P O Box 40
Madison, Indiana 47250-0040 U.S.A.

Email: JimWortham123@gmail.com

Autographed books may be ordered
direct from author.
See page 137 for order information.

The Summer of Love

Art via Unsplash, Pixabay
Editor & typesetter: Gypsy Mercer
Book and Cover Design: Gypsy Mercer

Excerpts by permission of author and publisher:
Love Touching Love/Jim Wortham
Touching You Touching Me/Jim Wortham
Loving You/Jim Wortham

Author's note: This is a work of fiction. Names, characters, places and incidents are a product of the author's imagination. Any resemblance to actual people, living or dead, or actual events is purely coincidental.

The Summer of Love/Jim Wortham ~ First Edition
ISBN 978-1928877202

Library of Congress Control Number: 2020915603

Dedication

TO WAITRESSES and BARTENDERS
of cafes, coffee shops and sports bars
who gave me lots of napkins
to write poems
for books I said
I would someday publish

TO MY DOG TIPPY
who hung out with me
and never complained
about anything I did

TO ALL WHO WROTE TO ME
after reading my books
thank you for your kindness
and encouragement
You are the reason
I am writing again

ENJOY

The Summer of Love

This is my diary

From beginning
to end,
you will see
  love beginning,
  love growing,
and
  love fading away

Like all my experiences
with love,
this one ended

I went to the beach
to be alone

I had given up on love
it never does last anyway
or so I thought

So I decided
to spend my days
on the beach
to help heal my broken heart

This is the way it was
when I looked up
and saw you walking toward me
licking a
     chocolate
     ice cream cone

You glanced my way

smiled

stopped to talk

At that time

I knew

love had come again

I did not know what to say
I mean
I knew all the lines like
Baby, what's happening
or
Let's groove together

But for some reason
I knew
those words would not
win an evening with you

Without planning it
I said
Do you want a coke?
You smiled big
it was then I knew
I had said the right thing

I became jealous
when you talked about
     Bach
     Mozart
     The Beatles
     Bob Dylan
and you said
My first love is music

You told me
how much you would give
just to see the folk singers
performing nearby

Didn't you know
I was suffering
from an inferiority complex
just being a
Love Poet
and nothing more
?

As I waited for you today
I decided to write my thoughts
on paper
so I could read them to you
This is what I wrote

I like you because
You have a beautiful smile
You have a cute laugh
You make me happy
You allow me to be myself
You like ice cream and so do I

Today I took

your wallet size photo

to the printer

I had it made

into a giant wall poster

After I put the poster

on my wall

I spent the night

looking at it

When you came
running into my arms
this morning
I was not surprised to smell
peanut butter and grape jam
on your breath

After all anyone who likes
     chocolate ice cream
      strawberries
      and me
is bound to enjoy eating
peanut butter
and grape jam sandwiches
once in a while

When you gave me
the painting you made
I remember turning it
upside down and sideways
When I asked
what it was
You turned quickly
so I could not see the tears
running down your face

I am sorry
I really do like the painting
I hung it
on the ceiling of my room

I have been tempted
to open your diary
when you leave your room
to get us cokes and cookies

After you leave your room
I pick up your diary
but always put it down
without opening it

I need the mystery
of not knowing
everything you think
and you need your secrets

Our best times together
are not the days we plan in detail
but those days we leave unplanned

I call them empty days
because we fill them up
with things we enjoy most
like trips to the sunshine shop
for lunch
and a tasty ice cream parlor
for supper

In the evenings
we spend our time
looking in bookstores
or listening to folk singers
in the park

I can try forever
to fix a cheese and bologna
     sandwich
but it never comes out as good
as those you make

I tried all day
to fix something I could eat

Either the food is no good
or I miss you so much
my appetite is gone

Today
you did not
smile

Your words
do not include
the two
of us
anymore

Is this
my imagination
or is it
a hint
of what is
to come
?

I remember you once saying
that the three little words
I love you
were easy to say
but hard to keep on meaning
    Were you
    trying to
    tell me
    something
    then
      ?

The

words

finally came

You said

your love

for me

had faded away

You offered

no

explanation

If our lives
together
must end
then
go quickly now
as I turn my head
to look at the sunset

When you leave
I will be looking at the
     red
     yellow
     blue
colors in the sky

After enjoying the sunset
I will look back at you
but you will be gone
I will look back at the sunset
and the colors of that sunset
will be gone too

And so another day is gone
And so another love is gone

I should have known
that anything good
must come
to an end

That beauty
fades away

That love
is illusive

I
should
have known

You offered
all the love
you knew how to give

And as
quickly as you came
into my life
you were
gone

Letters

First meeting

My hand
reaches for
your hand

You accept
my touch

I speak
of love
you respond

It seems
we have known
each other
forever

Gypsy girl
your mysterious aura
makes you exotic
Men are afraid
to ask you for a date
They think
you will say
NO

Gypsy girl
your beauty
keeps you lonely

You are Gone

You spoke
of
love

And I
believed
you

Now
you
are gone

This
is how
it always is

An Endless Day

When I am with you

it is like

a magic day

without beginning

or end

Trapped in a Box

I keep souvenirs
of our dates
in a box

Concert ticket stubs
Dried roses
Napkins
Shell earrings
Love letters

Daily I look through my box
dreaming of our good times
but find life's meaning
slowly fading
now that you are gone

My life
is trapped
in a box

Movie Dinner You

Was it the movie
that made me happy

Or was it
the dinner?

Neither
It was you

First Week

I was careful

not to speak too soon

nor touch too fast

My thoughts said

move slowly

No Romance

If our relationship
is not to evolve
beyond friendship
I must accept this

Pretty Butterflies

Once upon a time

A pretty girl
in the park
painted lovely things
     giant butterflies
     yellow roses
     the sun
     the moon
She tried
to capture in symbolic form
concepts of love

Encountering her
I decided that
real love
Hers and mine
Could be better than
capturing abstract love

So I asked her
for a walk in the park
we held hands
we laughed
we hugged
This was the beginning
of love

No longer does she need
to capture love
in those mysterious forms
She now has real love
to experience
and paint

Her paintings
were more beautiful
her art more real

Coke Dates

Too much money
is spent
impressing
a new girl

Either she likes you
or doesn't

Money shouldn't enter in
Coke dates can be perfect

A Poetess I Never Knew
or
Goodnight, Poetess

I read about you
The pages draw me
into your world of love
joy and excitement

At night
I dream
about spending
a lifetime with you

Sometime,
maybe tomorrow
I must realize
that a dream
is only a dream

I must also realize
that I will
only know you
by the pages in your book

Good night
Poetess

You and I

I want to be with you often
but I have no money
to take you to movies
or fancy restaurants
but I can bring you
colorful flowers
from my yard
For dinner
I can offer you peanut butter
and grape jam sandwiches
and whatever you want to drink
In the evenings
we can take long walks
through the park
stop along the way
share words of love
return home
and discover more about each other
while talking by candle light
Then you will realize
how special you are
  to me

Try to Understand

I like
quiet times
not wild parties

I like
soft music
not blaring sounds

I desire
honesty
not games

I desire
warmth
not indifference

Please try
to understand
me

Hints

How could you dance

into my life

with hints of love

and then leave

never to come

before my eyes again

?

Sorry

I am sorry
I ignored
your
silent cries
for help

Busy days
school
sports
work
drowned your voice

I have neglected you
my friend
I am sorry

Being Me

I will not try
to impress you

I believe
being natural
is a treasure

Look at me
you will find beauty

One Milkshake, Please

Two straws
and

one
milkshake

is
enough

for
Lovers

You are so Beautiful

You are one of those
beautiful people

When I see you
I smile
and feel happy inside

So Tired

I am

tired of

studying

I need

to share

this night

with someone

Tomorrow

I sit watching
the clock take me
closer to tomorrow

Bad because
I have many things
to do

Good because
there is so much
to enjoy

Moon Power

The moon is his strength
I have seen him
     weak
     slumping from lack of sleep
     hungry
     unloved

It was not always so
Recently I saw him
     dancing on the beach
          like a young boy
Tonight he is crawling
     to the surf
He looks at the moon
     energy flows into his body
     his body strengthens

What happens
I don't know
the moon is his strength
One day he will be a legend

A Poem for Estella

Wherever you

are

remember

we loved

one

summer

Paths

Your path
and mine
have never
crossed

It is
now time
for us
to meet

Last Night's Delight

You came into my life
when I needed someone
We sat
listened to records
talked
I shared with you
some of my dreams
as I listened to you
I found myself dreaming again
listening to your laugh
Sometimes
I tried to imagine
what you were thinking
It was late
we had to part
I saw in your eyes
that we should be together again

Sophistication

When I return to simplicity
and act on compulsion
people say
I'm acting unsophisticated

To be okay means
    to be detached
    unemotional

Do not return to simplicity
my friend
If you do
you will not be okay

Numbers

Each phone number
I dial

Busy
No answer
Sorry she moved away
Oh she is married
The number you dialed
     is now disconnected

And the night goes on
     in circles
     of endless numbers

I would talk to myself
but even my mind
got up and walked out
     of the room
looking for some activity

Dreams

People say
You are living in a dream world
You talk of being an actress
     writing a novel
     driving a jeep
     living on the beach
No one listens
They say you are dreaming
They call you a child

I will tell you
There is magic in the air
Your dreams can come true
If you need help
      someone will come running

This is a beautiful world
     for anyone who dares to dream
Reach for those dreams today
Someone will be there
     to help you too

When in Love

When I am
in love
everything
about life
falls into place

When I
am not
in love
nothing about
life
seems right

Walking

I go out
and walk

If anyone asks
I will tell them
I'm looking for someone
who might offer kindness

No one asks that question
No one is outside

There is nobody to talk with
There is nothing to do
There is nothing else to be said

Yes and No

I change
this is my right

I am
the sum
of my experiences

Today I
say yes
when yesterday
I said no

Today I
say no
when yesterday
I said yes

This is my right
I change

Memories

When you are away
I close my eyes
recall our yesterdays
and

touch

your

hand

The Temple

Lady
at the temple
I adore you

When you smile
love flows
from your presence

I watch
as you
pray

Beautiful lady
touch me
with your peace

Masks

Your mask is hiding
a real person
One who
dreams
loves
hurts
You hope
someone
will accept
and love you
Only then
will you be able
to take off
your mask

My Response to Masks

It is okay to wear masks
Sometimes cruel people
     will hurt you
Do not expose yourself
     to everyone
People do not know
     how to react
          to a real person
Walk carefully

Love Circles

I will love again
I always do

I will care again
too soon

Love will end again
it always does

The Night the Laughter Died

It happened one Friday night
    at Pizza Hut
shapely girls with their
    long hair
    faded jeans
came to meet the guys
after the football game

One football player bragged
    about sex
Another told about a car
    he had stolen
They all told their stories
They all laughed

A football quarterback
named Bill
said something different
I used to be on drugs
I had sex with anyone I wanted
I did anything for an ego trip

The Summer of Love

The air got heavy
There was no plastic in his voice

Everyone knew
he was telling the truth
He kept speaking
Jesus gave me peace
I don't need those things anymore

No one chuckled
eyes were fastened on Bill

Now I have a continuous joy
since I asked Jesus into my life
Bill said no more
He looked down at the floor

One by one
the teenagers closed their eyes
in silent meditation
One by one
they found they needed only Jesus
to satisfy their longings in life
I was there
I know

Go Away

I tried
to forget
you

Thoughts
invaded
my privacy

and
reminded
me
of you

Discovery

The problem
is not
the inability
to communicate

It is not
discovering
other ways
to communicate

but rather
not wanting to

I Can/You Can

Poets and artists
are not the only people
who desire to be creative
Within each of us
there is a need
to create something
that brings joy to others
Do not say
you have no opportunity
Use what you have
You will attract
everything you need
to spread love
and beauty to others

Vacation Romances

I love vacation romances
You meet
You touch
Inhibitions
are left at home

Just the two of you
sharing laughter
and carefree days

Vacation romances
are short enough
to be perfect

Tea

Sipping tea
is how we will spend
tonight
Free
Easy
We like it this way

You Left

When you discovered
I was a person
with imperfections
like yours

You became
disinterested
and
left

Silent Words

When we first met
could you
read my mind
when I was thinking
"I love you"
?

A Perfect Day

The wind
loosens your hair
as it blows
across your face

You hum
sweetly
while we walk

Time slows down
and
love encircles us

Questions Need Answers

The question is
Where do I fit in
?

Am I at the top
or the bottom
of your list
?

Please give me
a special place
in your dreams

Without Warning

You said something wrong
Unnecessary
Yes
But it was said

Our relationship
crumbled
before our eyes
as tension
charged the after air

And in silence
you
and
I
walked away

in different directions

A Touch of Silence

Silence is needed
There is a special kind of love
that comes from
looking
into each other's eyes
and touching hands

Paradise

My

paradise

is

found

wherever

you

happen

to be

The Last Night

Our last night
together
is here

I
will not
cry

There will be
too much time
for crying
later

Single Living

You say
the single life
is wonderful

All that free love
no responsibility
going wherever you desire

If single living
is so great
why do I hear
you crying
when I pass
your apartment
?

Search

I will search
for love
A voice
deep inside
tells me
there is
someone
for me

Each Day

During each minute

of each day

remember

You

are

loved

Privacy

I must go
    but I will return

I must be alone
    at times

Please do not
    invade my privacy

Aloneness
    is a part
        of me

I will be back

Sea Shells
&
Love

When I Love

When I love
I write happy poems

When love is
over
I write sad poems

When love
is neither
now
or over
I rearrange my poems

When I am tired
of rearranging
I get on my knees
and pray
for love

Waiting

For all who are
waiting for love
to happen

I sometimes
find it
helpful
to sleep
until
the pain of
no one
being there
is over

and if that
takes
too long

I comb my hair
put on clothes
walk out of my room
and
let love happen

The Message

A young girl
sits beneath a tree
tracing a design into the dirt
with her small finger
She looks into the sky
then across the fields
then back to the sky again
thinking about the young soldier
she had been waiting for
until today

Say

Say that you are
lonely
and want someone
to be with

Say that you are
helpless
and need someone
to be there

Say that you are
uncertain
and need someone
to understand you

Circles

Once if this had happened
I would have tried
to figure out
what I said
or what I did wrong

That is all right
if you enjoy going around
in circles

But after a while
circles get boring
and you get nowhere
except where you
began

So I've learned
to let the past
take care of itself
while I enjoy
the now

IF

If
lovers
could
love
without
analyzing
what the other
means
with each word
or
action

If
lovers
could
love
without
asking
about
the
past or future

then
love
could
be

WHY

Now that I am alone
what happened
between
when love
began
and
now

I know
you change
but why
And why so fast
And why so soon
?

Yesterday was good
I had no reason
to question
today
Perhaps I should have

Maybe

I did not know
loving you
could be so much fun

I did not know
not loving you
could be so bad

Maybe
you will
come back

Maybe
you won't

What will I do
if
you
do not
?

You

The nights
are getting longer
and much cooler
This afternoon
while driving in my car
I turned to say
something
to you
but you were not there

Pizza Hut

Our first date
was simple
We decided to get
to know
each other
so we went to Pizza Hut
We ate a cheese pizza
drank two cokes
I often think
about
those teenagers who
came to our table
and asked if we were
Jesus People

I asked
why
It is because of your love
they said

This is how
I remember
our first date

Secrets are Secrets

I
shared
too
much

Secrets
are made
to be
secrets

You needed mystery
You said
Goodbye
I shared
too
much

Dancing

Do you remember
dancing
on the island
where
     eyes
     and
     feelings
     spoke
That night
became a snapshot
I look at
often

Years have passed
Do you remember
dancing
        ?

Touch

The first touch
of a warm hand
on my hand
is beautiful

The last touch
knowing it is
going to be the last
touch
is tragic
but always happens

There is a hope
in everyone
I think
that says
it really does not have
to be that way

Until that time
and place
let me hold your hand
The love now is worth
the hurt later

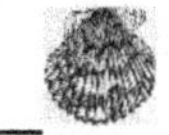

You Came Running

You invaded
my life
with
love
concern
touch
I need you
this morning
I asked
God
for a happy day
and
you
came
running

No Smile

Yesterday
I called out to you
but you were silent
I pretended it did not matter

Today I smiled
as you walked past
Then a cold wind
slapped me in the face

Tomorrow
I will find
it hard
to look
in your direction

Careful

Be careful
not to rearrange me
into your idea
of a perfect person
I have traits
that you do not like
I know that
What you consider bad
others might like
Allow me to remain
the person
I am

Invasion

Allow me
to enter your world
We can let our eyes meet
and laugh together
We can let our hands
touch
with warmth
We can bring
our lives
together
and
     dream
          hope
               care
          wish
     plan
love

Let us
invade
each other's world
and make them
into one

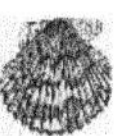

Loving was Made to be Simple

You say
I am easy to know
because I like
simple things
I say
that is the only way
two people can
learn to love
Let us simplify ourselves
and care
and touch
and listen
and be
Loving
was made
to be simple

I am Tender

They talked about

cheating

grades

getting a job

college

becoming successful

being respectable

Can't they see

I need love

Love that will stay

during the years

of growing up

Mood Swings

Some days

I feel so certain

of myself

Today

I feel

I must change

I spoke to someone

but he kept walking

I need

someone

to tell me

I am okay

Let me Tell You a Secret

If we are together
and I lean forward
it means I like you

If a smile
stays on my face
it means you can
affect my feelings

I trust you
or
I would not
have told you
these things

I Was

I was desiring
    your love

I was dreaming
    of a lifetime with you

I was in love
    with you

I was happy
    until you left

I was

Visions of You

Believe me when I say
I think of you often
No one is like you

The way you are
is exactly what I like

You are beautiful
The fact that
you do not think so
makes you more beautiful

I can laugh
or act anyway I want
I can act like a little kid
and you will act
that way too

Talking with you
was always something
I looked forward to
even on the telephone

When we were together
everything around us
faded away
There was only room
for the two of us
Did I ever tell
you that
    ?

I will remember you
this way unless
our lives touch again
Then the next poem
may be different

Time Piece

I was just
something
to pass
your time
until the
perfect guy
came along

It was all right
for you to spend
your time that way
but you had
no right
to waste
my life

A Poet

I could never
write a poem
until
you touched
my life
with love

At
that moment
a Poet
was born

Always

No matter
what happens
between us
this is the way
it will
always be

When
I think of you
I will think
of myself
and when I think
of myself
I will
think of you

Close to Me

Everything
in this mixed up world
seems
all right
when you
are
close to me

Come
be
close to me
forever

Strawberry Soda

We do simple things
like drinking
strawberry soda
    with two straws
going out on the ocean
    with an inflatable raft
pretending we are
looking for a new continent
    to discover

Faded Blue Jeans

It amazes me
that no matter if you wear
faded blue jeans
or one of your
bright colorful dresses
you always look beautiful

It seems as if
every word you say
builds me into more
of a man

If ever
two people
were meant
for each other
we are

A Magic Spell

You have cast
a magic spell on me
I have found myself
looking only at you
like an art collector
who has found
a rare painting

I almost
gave up on love
Then you touched
my life
And for that
I will always
be thankful

A Moment of Love

I
prefer
lasting love
Someday
I believe
it may come

But
today
I need love
even if it
is for
a moment

Magic of Yesterdays

Bring back the days
when I could listen to rainbows
talk to the grass
and make every rock my friend

Things seemed bigger and better
Sitting on the grass
was sometimes more fun
than going to school
I played hooky then
The sunshine talked to me
It kept me company
At night the stars sang
They don't anymore

I ate hot dogs because
they weren't good for me
and candy
when my mom was not looking
She let me do that

Once I wrote poems to a girl
I dreamed of being Shakespeare
and I was
for awhile

I want to feel
hear
see
need
again

I once needed baseball cards
and puppy dogs
I now need someone
Someone to love
Someone to care

Go Easy

Go easy
into your
next romance

Relax
Enjoy
Don't rush

If nothing more
than friendship
arises
remember
that a friend
is a
beautiful thing

Castles

I talked
about building
castles
on the sand
You talked
about
building castles
in the sky
using
us
as the
building blocks

After thinking
for a moment
and realizing
that your kind
of castles
last longer
I said
So when do we begin
?

Without Games

I watch others
playing games
Playing
hard to get
or
trying to impress
each other

I am tired of games
I do not want to
waste the time

Will anyone come
without games
?

Candy Flavored Lipstick

You wear
  warm smiles
  twinkling eyes
  love perfume
  candy flavored lipstick

Thank you
for wearing them

A Long Night

I drop a dime
into the telephone
to call you

No answer

Every ten minutes
I call

When darkness
fills the sky
I will know
the
longest night
of my life
has begun

Tic Toc

Today

I had

a steady stream

of inspiration

I thought of you

every time

my watch ticked

OCEAN

Remember
the
ocean waves
and the sand

We talked
and
became friends

Soft kisses
gone now
yet
remembered

Will I
ever
see you
again
?

If not
take me
back to
the ocean

Let
me
start
again

Thank you

Thank you
for making me
thick vanilla milk shakes
while I made
oil paintings
of lovers
on the beach

Did I ever tell you
that I loved
the brownies
you made
?

You always
made me smile
when things
were not going well

I appreciate
you
more than
you will ever know

Cheri

It was
your talent
to do
all the things
that made me
smile

Fun Filled Days

You
never ask
about my past
or future
You live
only for the now
You always say
Yesterday is gone
and
tomorrow
has yet to come

You explore
all there is
in each moment
Because of this
my days
have been filled
with
magic moments
that will last
forever

Alone

During the
in-between days
of no love
my eyes become alert
for the slightest hint
of any
who might
offer
love

Rainbow

You are like a rainbow
colorful
forever changing
to as many moods
as there are colors
in a rainbow
One day you are sad
One day you are happy
One night you are in love
with the moon
One night you are
casting wishes upon a star
Your moods change
making you beautiful
like a rainbow

Sometimes

Sometimes

I can sense

that a love relationship

is over

Last night

was one of those times

Looking Back

Looking back

I realize

the little things

about you

that once annoyed me

have been forgotten

All I remember

is the fun we had

Kite

The string snapped

I watched my kite

sail to the sky

You came running

with tears in your eyes

saying

I saw what happened

I am sorry

Even though

I did not know you

the moment

was magic

A Giant Strawberry

Sometimes

you

are funny

Do you remember

the morning

you took

a giant red strawberry

and put whipped cream

on top of it

?

It tasked

good

Didn't it

?

Take My Hand

Take my hand
Stand by
me

I
will become
all that
I
was created
to be

I Will Take Your Hand

I will
take
your hand

I will
stand
by you

You will
become
all that
you were
created to be

Color Photo

I will mentally

photograph this moment

Soon it will be over

I will constantly

recall this photo

and study every detail

What Do You Think

I
still believe
two can
live happily

That
one can
keep the interest
of the other

What
do
you
think
?

The Seasons of Love Series

The Summer of Love $ 9.95

The Autumn of Love $ 9.95

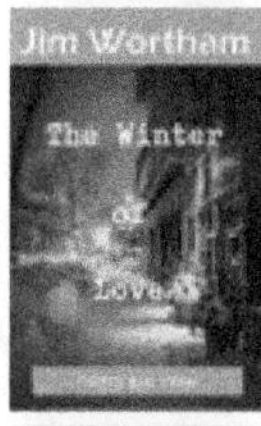

The Winter of Love $ 9.95

The Spring of Love $ 9.95

Thank you for reading my book.
Autographed copies are available from
Jim Wortham, PO Box 40
Madison, Indiana 47250-0040 U.S.A.
Email: Jim Wortham123@gmail.com

Shipping within the United States is
$5 for the entire order. Contact me
for overseas shipping costs.

Follow Jim Wortham

Jim's blog: www.JimWorthamPoet.com
Facebook: www.facebook.com/Jim.Wortham.54
Jim's email: jimwortham123@gmail.com

Jim Wortham Poetry Books
Post Office Box 40
Madison, Indiana 47250-0040
U.S.A.

Autographed books available

www.ingramcontent.com/pod-product-compliance
Lightning Source LLC
Chambersburg PA
CBHW031515040426
42445CB00009B/239

* 9 7 8 1 9 2 8 8 7 7 2 0 2 *